UNDERSTANDING YOU

UNDERSTANDING EMOTIONS

by Elizabeth Andrews

Cody Koala
An Imprint of Pop!
popbooksonline.com

abdobooks.com
Published by Pop!, a division of ABDO, PO Box 398166, Minneapolis, Minnesota 55439.

Printed in the United States of America, North Mankato, Minnesota

052022
092022

THIS BOOK CONTAINS RECYCLED MATERIALS

Cover Photo: Shutterstock Images
Interior Photos: Shutterstock Images, GettyImages

Editor: Grace Hansen
Series Designer: Victoria Bates

Library of Congress Control Number: 2021951834

Publisher's Cataloging-in-Publication Data
Names: Andrews, Elizabeth, author.
Title: Understanding emotions / by Elizabeth Andrews
Description: Minneapolis, Minnesota : Pop, 2023 | Series: Understanding you | Includes online resources and index
Identifiers: ISBN 9781098242138 (lib. bdg.) | ISBN 9781644948491 (pbk.) | ISBN 9781098242831 (ebook)
Subjects:LCSH: Human emotions--Juvenile literature. | Feelings--Juvenile literature. | Social interaction-- Juvenile literature. | Interpersonal relations--Juvenile literature.
Classification: DDC 152.4--dc23

Hello! My name is

Cody Koala

Pop open this book and you'll find QR codes like this one, loaded with information, so you can learn even more!

Scan this code* and others like it while you read, or visit the website below to make this book pop.

popbooksonline.com/emotions

*Scanning QR codes requires a web-enabled smart device with a QR code reader app and a camera.

Table of Contents

Chapter 1

Understanding Emotions

Understanding your own emotions can help you build positive relationships with friends and family. It's important to learn how to **identify** and **express** your feelings.

Watch a video here!

Chapter 2

Learning about Emotions

When emotions come up, talk about them with adults around you. Grown-ups have **experience** understanding emotions, so they can help you learn about your own.

Learn more here!

Isaac's family is about to leave for vacation. His heart is beating fast and he can't sit still. He asks his dad why his body is acting this way. Isaac's dad tells him he is feeling excitement.

Your heartbeat can get faster when you are feeling nervous, excited, or afraid.

Chapter 3

It's How You Feel

The emotions you feel affect the way you act. If you are sad, you may frown or cry. You might not want to play with friends. It's okay to let people know you need a break.

Explore links here!

Maya had a busy day at school. At dinner, her sister takes the slice of pizza Maya wanted. She feels so angry that she cries. Emotions feel more **intense** when people are tired.

If you get upset when things do not go your way, you are feeling frustrated.

It just snowed in Jane's town. She is out sledding with her friends. They all

laugh and smile while they fly down the hill. They are happy!

Chapter 4

Other People's Emotions

When you know how to **identify** your own emotions, you can help others with their feelings too. It makes you a better friend.

Complete an activity here!

anger

happiness

surprise

fear

sadness

disgust

There are ways to check in on other people's emotions. One is asking, "how are you feeling?" Sometimes a person can tell you how they are feeling without words. Pay attention to their **body language**, facial expressions, and **tone** of voice.

Ella rubs her hands together before she starts her animal presentation for class. Henry knows this is a sign that Ella is nervous. He gives Ella a thumbs up and a smile to help her feel more **confident**.

Making Connections

Text-to-Self

Do you talk about your emotions with an adult? If so, have they given you good advice?

Text-to-Text

Have you read any other books about feelings? What did they have in common with this book?

Text-to-World

What do you think needs to change in daily life for people to feel more comfortable expressing their emotions?

Glossary

body language – gestures or movements that can communicate how a person is feeling.

confident – feeling sure of one's own ability.

experience – skills or knowledge people get by doing something.

express – to show.

identify – to find out what something is.

intense – deeply felt.

tone – the sound of words as they show a feeling.

Index

Online Resources

popbooksonline.com

Thanks for reading this Cody Koala book!

Scan this code* and others like it in this book, or visit the website below to make this book pop!

popbooksonline.com/emotions

*Scanning QR codes requires a web-enabled smart device with a QR code reader app and a camera.